SOMEONE COULD WIN A POLAR BEAR

SOMEONE COULD
WIN A POLAR BEAR

JOHN CIARDI

DRAWINGS BY EDWARD GOREY

J.B. LIPPINCOTT COMPANY PHILADELPHIA NEW YORK

ACKNOWLEDGMENT
Some of these poems were first published in
Saturday Review.

For Paula Danziger, whose classroom
is a happy place for poetry—and to all
her students, present and to come,
who will learn to be good readers because
she taught them to enjoy reading.

CONTENTS

SOMEONE COULD WIN A POLAR BEAR

Someone Could Win a Polar Bear

I met a Polar Bear among the floes.
He was all Polar Bear down to his toes.
Also from side to side and tail to nose.

He was all Polar Bear from roar to roar.
Sometimes at sixty miles an hour, or more.
I know for certain he was not much slower.

For I was going south after we met,
And doing all of sixty, you can bet,
And still I felt his breathing, hot and wet.

And all because I had stepped on his toe.
I said, "I'm sorry, sir. I didn't know
You were a bear. I thought you were just snow!"

I said it as politely as I could.
Somehow I felt he had misunderstood.
And I'm afraid his manners were not good.

He roared what sounded something like "Good-bye!"
And so I left. At first I wondered why
He was still there. I wasn't. Jets don't fly

As fast as I was leaving. Still that bear
I thought I'd left kept right on being there.
He had a way of being everywhere.

Or just one step behind. I ran all day
And still that bear stayed just one step away.
Why would he roar good-bye and then just stay?

I ran all night, all week, all month, all year.
I'm running still and still that bear is here.
I have a feeling that the end is near,

But don't know how to end it. All I know
Is: I don't want the bear to. If I go
Around in circles for an hour or so

Will someone think and tell me what to do?
Now don't be hasty: think your answer through.
Someone could win a Polar Bear.—Maybe you!

Rules

Whatever way a thing is done
    Is wrong, as I hope you know.
For that is the rule of One times One.
    It's the way things always go.

It can't be helped and there's nothing to do
    Except (as you'll discover)
By the ancient rule of Two times Two,
    Which is: *First, do it over.*

And to do it over, as you must see,
    Means first you must do it wrong.
That's where we come to rule Three times Three:
    Improve as you go along.

If you get it right, right off the bat,
    That ends it right away.
What's left to do when you've done that?
    You've wasted the whole day!

No boy who starts by doing it wrong
    Is finished early, is he?
And if he improves it all day long,
    Why, then, his whole day's busy.

Then everything's proper, do you see?
    For idleness is to deplore.
Don't be right till it's time to be.
    That is the rule of Four times Four.

The Blabberhead

The Blabberhead is blubbery.
His face is full of shrubbery.
His neck is long and rubbery.

So is his nose. That nose of his
Is blue and sticks out of his fizz
Into whatever's not his biz—

I mean his *business*. What is not
His business is, well, quite a lot.
In fact, most everything. But wot—

I mean *what* makes the Blabber one
Most systematically to shun
Is that the instant he is done

Sticking his nose into affairs
He sticks it out again, and stares,
And gives himself all sorts of airs.

Then, grabbing everyone's lapel,
He starts to tell and tell and tell.
Worse yet, he doesn't tell it well.

He blabbers, blubbers, blurts, and fizzes.
He rattles off the that's and this's.
Whatever business isn't his is

All his business. In he charges
Like a river full of barges,
And (to say the least) enlarges

On whatever he can pick up.
Then, as like as not, he'll hiccup
Eat your cake, and break the teacup,

While that bright blue nose of his,
Sticking out of his mad fizz,
Sniffs so that it makes you diz—

I mean *dizzy*. Yammer, clatter!
Here he is! There goes the platter!
Here comes gossip—splutter, splatter!

You can see from what I've said
The manners of the Blabberhead
Are of a sort you well may dread.

Avoid, abstain from, shun, eschew
False blabbering (or even true),
Or you may soon discover *you*

Are growing loud and blubbery
With a face all full of shrubbery,
And a neck too long and rubbery,

And (as your nose turns blue)
That a universal snubbery
Will certainly ensue.

The Answer

A man I knew met a man he knew.
A man who knows us all
Asked them to ask me to ask you
If it is Spring or Fall.

It happened one man was not free,
So only one came by.
He made me a firm promise he
Would pass on your reply.

I told him to tell him to tell
The one who asked to know,
I did not know you very well
But I'd ask my wife to go.

You told her to tell him to tell
One man to tell the other,
You hoped that he was feeling well,
And that you'd ask your mother.

I'm told she told you to tell her
She didn't care to know.
And I told him to tell him, sir,
To tell him she said so.

He told him to tell him to say
To me, through her, to you,
He'll call on her himself today
To ask if it is true.

21

The Lesson

Of all the fleas that ever flew
(And flying fleas are rather few
((Because for proper flying you
(((Whether you are a flea or not)))
Need wings and things fleas have not got)))—

(I make the further point that fleas
Are thick as these parentheses
((An illustration (((you'll agree)))
Both apt and pleasing to a flea)))—

Now then where were we? Let me see—
Ah, yes. —We said to fly you ought
(Whether you are a flea or not)
To have some wings (yes, at least two
((At least no less than two will do
(((And fleas have something less than one
((((One less, in fact (((((or, frankly, none)))))
((((((Which, as once more you will agree))))))
Limits the flying of a flea)))))))))).

And let me add that fleas that fly
Are known as Flears. (You can see why.)

All I have said thus far is true.
(If it's not clear, that's up to you.
((You'll have to learn sometime, my dear,
That what is true may not be clear
(((While what is clear may not be true
((((And you'll be wiser when you do.))))))))))

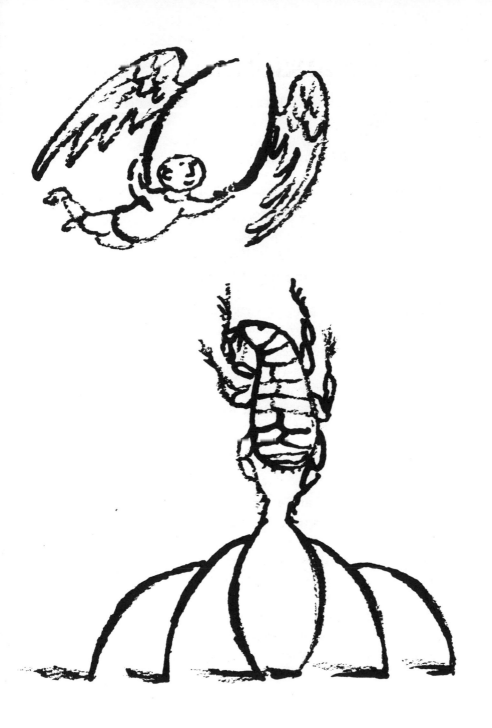

Good and Bad Habits
(They are sometimes mixed.)

There once were two slovenly chaps
Who spilled half their food in their laps.
    Both laps (one apiece)
    Were soon covered with grease
In which were embedded odd scraps.

They became as unsightly as freaks
(And they reeked of sour cabbage and leeks).
    But one glance on the quiet
    Would tell you their diet
For at least the last fifty-two weeks.

I am glad they are not eating here.
But still, let me hope I've made clear
    They did keep close track
    Of things that went back
To last week, and last month, and last year.

Their method was poor of its kind.
But in general, I think, you will find
    (Though their way *was* inept)
    That a record well kept
Is the sign of a well-ordered mind.

Friendship

Willy the Weep and Sad Terry and I
Were sitting here thinking of you.
And Willy and Terry were having a cry.
And I was having one, too, I was.
For we knew it just had to be true, we did.
We knew it just had to be true.

Willy had hot dogs and Terry had toast
And I had a pail full of lunch.
But our tears came so hard and so fast (almost)
We sat there and just couldn't munch. (Not quite,
But *almost* we just couldn't munch.) Besides,
The tears were wetting our lunch.

Said Willy the Weep as he chewed and he cried,
"I cannot believe it is true!"
And Sad Terry said, "Pass the salt." And he sighed,
"I hate to believe it myself, I do. (Except
That, of course, it is perfectly true. Too bad.
But we all know it's perfectly true.)"

So I ate a pickle and Willy the Weep
Ate six and Sad Terry ate ten.
And we wept and we ate till we all fell asleep
In our sorrow, and oh, even then (alas)
We wept for you now and again, we did,
Till we woke and wept for you again.

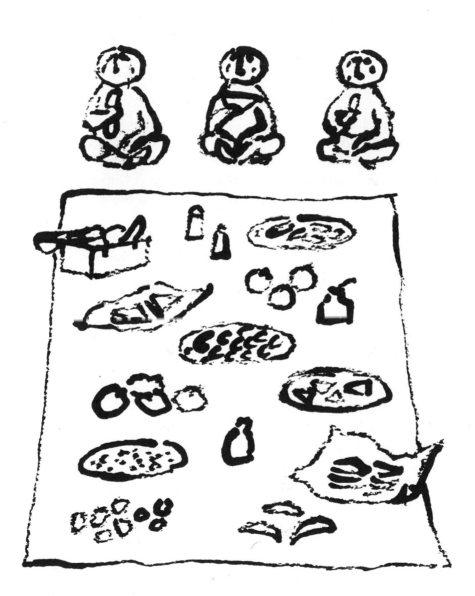

"But (please pass the mustard) just what did he do?"
Said Terry. "I have to agree
That whatever it was must be perfectly true,
Though I hate to believe it, for he (poor boy)
Is my friend. But, of course, I'll agree, I will,
If you will explain it to me."

"Oh, a terrible thing," said Willy, "and that
Is the whole truth. A terrible shame.
Though now that you ask, I don't know just what.
But a terrible thing all the same (I'm sure).
And though it's a terrible shame, I say,
He'll just have to shoulder the blame."

So Willy the Weep and Sad Terry and I
Were speaking in friendship of you.
And Willy and Terry were having a cry.
And I was having one, too, I was.
For we knew it just had to be true, we did.
We knew it just had to be true.

The Music Master

"My sons," said a Glurk slurping soup,
"We would make a fine musical group.
    Put your spoon to your lip
    And slurp when you sip,
But don't spill. Like this, children—*oop*!"

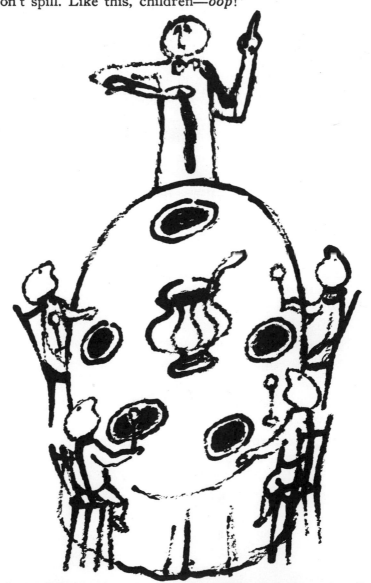

About Rivers and Toes

A river has a way to go.
The way it goes is—flow. It flows
Over (mostly) mud and (sometimes) toes.
It makes its own mud, as you know.
But it has to depend on luck for toes.
The reason is—it can't make those.

You have to make them and put them there.
The best way is to put them in bare
And (mostly) in summer. Unless you feel
You'd like to be—or are—a seal.
In that case, duck your toes when you please.
The cold will never make you sneeze.

—Except that a seal has no toes!

Now isn't that just how it goes?
It's the ones *without* toes that get
The best chance of getting them wet.
While we, if we put our toes in
When it's freezing will get them back frozen.

It's enough to make a man feel
He'd be better off as a seal.

But were he a seal, I suppose
He'd feel bad about not having toes.
It's a problem both ways, goodness knows.

But the problem of toes or no toes
Is nothing (as you might suppose)
To a river. The river just flows.

Still, it's good to have toes on your foot
(Or on both feet) for then you can put
One or all in the mud—go ahead.
Provided it's warm, as I said.

You *could* even put in your head.
I doubt the river would care:
It's going a long way from there.
But heads left too long
In a river go wrong:
They lose all the part in their hair.

Still (the point is) the river won't care.
It's going a long way from there.
All *it* cares to know
Is the best way to flow
Over mud, toes, the part in your hair,
Or anything else you could name.

To a river most things are the same.

About Moose

or,

To hairy cows, the hairy bull
Is handsomer than horrible

Bull moose are beastly and contrary,
Ornery, horned, humped-up, and hairy.
It seems hard to imagine how
A bull moose could attract a cow.
But every spring the mooselets come
To prove he must attract her some.
Perhaps because, though hornless, she
Is just as downright ornery
At times, and as humped-up as he.
She's just as hairy certainly.

Whatever it is that makes him seem
The answer to a girl-moose dream,
He's all the answer Mrs. Moose gets.
And every spring—here come the mooselets.

It seems just as mysterious
To ask what makes him serious
About her. But we must allow
Ladies their secrets. Anyhow,
There are the mooselets every spring.
Proving—if they prove anything—
It must be true what Noah knew
About the animals two by two.

However beastly and contrary,
Ornery, horned, humped-up, and hairy
Moose (bull or cow) may seem to be
To such non-moose as you and me,
Clearly whatever first made moose meant
To provide them some inducement
To shun mere sentimental looseness
And yearn for one another's mooseness.

Else mooselets would be far and few.
And so should I. And so would you.

The Hearsay

The Whispering Hearsay lives its life
    In far-off Wild Conjecture.
And there it weaves (so does its wife)
    Whole cloth of such poor texture
That anyone with half an eye
    Could certainly see through it,
Though if you ask the Hearsay why,
    It snarls back, "Could *you* do it?"

The Buffalo

The buffalo has a hump on top.
    He has a tail behind.
Once his stampedes were hard to stop.
    Now he is hard to find.

For centuries he ran and ran
    Across the golden plain.
He ran so fast that he began
    Not to come back again.

And where he ran for years and years
    The hunters of the Sioux
Twanged their bows and flung their spears
    And had a barbecue.

But the buffalo ran so fast so far
    That he ran clean away.
And that is why the sad Sioux are
    Eating less well today.

He ran away with his hump on top
    He ran with his tail behind.
And wherever he stopped (if he did stop)
    Now he is hard to find.

The Rover

(To be recited loud and with gestures)

The rover arrived at a river.
    The river arrived with a roar.
A ravine that the river had riven
    Made its roaring reverberate more.

The river raved so that the rover
    Reviled it. "Rave, river," said he.
"Though you rock the ravine you have riven,
    Your rage is no ravage to me!"

Thus ever the revenant rover
    Reverts to the rhetoric of man,
Than which, though it roar like a raver,
    What rock-wracking river's rage can?

Widgeonry

(And why *shouldn't* you use
your dictionary?)

A widgeon in a wicopy
In which no widgeon ought to be
A widowed widgeon was.

While in a willow wickiup
A Wichitaw sat down to sup
With other Wichitaws.

And what they whittled as they ate
Included what had been of late
A widgeon's wing. 'Twas thus

The widgeon in the wicopy
In which no widgeon ought to be
A widowed widgeon was.

Garden Notes
from Zanzibar

The roses down in Zanzibar
Refuse to grow where pansies are.
Nor will the pansies, one supposes,
Consent to grow among the roses.

But, more remarkable by far,
Most zinnias in Zanzibar
Grow not at all, or grow so sparsely
They look like sprigs of sickly parsley.

They grow so thinly and so poorly
One cries, "Those can't be zinnias, surely!"
There is no flower that grows as skinny as
What Zanzibarians call zinnias.

The Whatchamacallit

There once was a Thingumajig.
Like a Whatsis, but three times as big.
    When it first came in view
    It looked something like you,
But it stayed and turned into a pig.

Four Things to Note about a Goat

Four things about a Billy Goat
Are: first, string whiskers on his throat.
Well, on his chin then. Sure enough
They *start* on his chin, though where they *leave off*
It's mostly throat. Though with a goat
The whiskers on its chin or throat
Just keep on going. Well, we'll say chin:
That seems a fair place to begin.

The second thing you will do well
To note about a goat is—smell.
Though even my aunts (who are so genteel
They shy away from anything real)
Are willing (on hot days) to think
Goats don't smell so much as stink.
Smell or stink, when you're near a goat,
Its odor is a thing you'll note.

That's two things, then. I'd say the third
Is how goats make a single word
Say everything they have to say.
They can make "Baaaah!" mean "Come and play!"
Or "Look at me!" or "Stay away!"
It's how they sing it—fast or slow,
Or loud or soft, or high or low—
That tells you what you need to know.

Take my advice: Don't go near goats
Till you know *all* the different notes
The Billy sings, or else Thing Four
About a goat will leave you sore
And stiff and sad. Thing Four, you'll note
(It's the goatiest thing about a goat)
Comes at you fast and knocks you flat.
(And the "Baaaah!" you hear then means "That's that!")

A Word about the True-Preposterous

The True-Preposterous is a beast
So much like any other
That to get born it needs at least
One father and one mother.

With parents properly arranged,
Preposteri (that's plural)
Appeared almost at once, and ranged
Through regions mostly rural.

Because, you see, when things began
Cities were somewhat fewer.
Preposteri since then, you can
Be absolutely sure,

Have gone to town. And you may meet
Most any day you're there, sir,
Preposterous herds along the street,
And in the park and square, sir.

More about Preposteri

Preposteri are born at birth.
They live a mortal span.
Their waists are equal to their girth.
They are seldom seen by man.

But children only need to sigh
And squinch their eyes and say the words.
And in come the Preposteri
In bands, and schools, and herds.

The Hairy-Nosed Preposterous

The Hairy-Nosed Preposterous
Looks much like a Rhinosterous,
But also something like a tank—
For which he has himself to thank.

His ears are the size of tennis shoes,
His eyes the size of pins.
And when he lies down for a snooze
An orchestra begins.

It whistles, rattles, roars, and thumps,
And the wind of it comes and goes
Through the storm-tossed hair that grows in clumps
On the end of his capable nose.

A Warning about the Preposterous

The Hairy-Nosed Preposterous
Is lost. His three fat tails
That should point where his master is
Are tangled in his scales.

He scratches with his hooves, which are
Made of the best molasses
(So they won't scratch or leave a scar
On the grasses when he passes).

He scratches, scratches, but, alas, his
Tails stick tighter.—As yours would
If you had hooves of fine molasses,
And three fat tails, and if you should

Try to scratch them free. I mean
Were you a Hairy-Nosed Preposterous
(Which is something in between
A Rhinoptamus and a Hipponosterous).

—You're not, of course. And well you may
Be glad of that. Now wash your ears
And go to bed and learn to say
Please and Thank you—or, my dears,

You may grow preposterous, too,
And have to go live at the zoo.

About Eskimos
(And why they wear pants)

The Eskimo wears pants because
  He makes them out of fur.
When he gets home he sits and thaws,
  And thaws his wife, and sings with her:
    Brrrr! Brrrr! Brrrr! Brrrr!

Some Eskimos are known to wear
  Pants made of seal. Others prefer
Walrus, snow fox, polar bear.
  But all of them wear fur.

A tailor for the Eskimo
  Must sew his pants up tight,
Or else when winds begin to blow
  The frost is apt to bite.

That's why the Eskimo wears pants
    Inside the pants he wears.
He's not inclined to take a chance
    With those sharp arctic airs.

The pants he wears inside the pants
    He wears are made of fur.
And—as you may see at a glance—
    The pants he wears *out*side are, sir.

Inside and out and all his life
    He wears his pants of fur.
So does—or so I'm told—his wife
    When he comes home and sings with her
      Brrrr! Brrrr! Brrrr! Brrrr!

One oddly gentle Eskimo
    Used seals but wouldn't skin 'em.
He thought that much too cruel, so
    His seal skins had seals in 'em.

The trouble was the seals grew fat
    Which made his pants grow tight.
Seals, moreover, bark. And that
    Kept him awake—six months a night.

Worse, when he took a step one way
    His pants would wriggle somewhere else.
His neighbors often stopped to say,
    "We recommend plain pelts."

Also, of course, he had to catch
  And feed his pants a lot of fish.
One day I saw his left leg snatch
  A trout right off the dish.

And worst of all, when he lay down
  To sleep, his pants inclined
To flip and flop and slip away.
  But still he didn't mind.

Not, that is, until one night
  When he was napping on his sled.
His left leg got into a fight
  With the right—and bit the thread!

Oh, what a scene! In my mind's eye
  (Except that my mind reels!)
I see his pants go slithering by—
  An unstitched pack of seals!

His outer pants, escaped, send back
  Their far, wild call. What hero
Could tame the wild blood of the pack?
  Ours feels a breeze (well below zero).

He sees more seals go slithering free.
  By putting two and two together
He need not even look to see
  Why he so feels the weather!

See, see our hero in the throes
Of passion, but too short of clothes
To mount a hot pursuit of those
Ungrateful pants. Too well he knows
That they are gone among the floes.
Gone! Gone! All gone! And the wind blows.
He feels a coldness in his toes.
He stomps, but still the coldness grows.
Next morning passing Eskimos
Remark, "He's friz!—Or is it 'froze'?"
—Their grammar, as you might suppose,
Is shaky. But the question shows
They think about it.—Friz or froze,
They bury him among the snows,
And leave him there. And each man goes

Back home just part friz—(froze?)—because
  His pants are made of fur—skinned fur.
And each man of them sits and thaws,
  And thaws his wife, and sings with her:
    Brrrr! Brrrr! Brrrr! Brrrr!